Copyright 2016 - All rig

MW01280156

This document is geared towards providing exact and reliable information in regards to the topic and issue covered. The publication is sold on the idea that the publisher is not required to render an accounting, officially permitted, or otherwise, qualified services. If advice is necessary, legal or professional, a practiced individual in the profession should be ordered.

From a Declaration of Principles which was accepted and approved equally by a Committee of the American Bar Association and a Committee of Publishers and Associations.

In no way is it legal to reproduce, duplicate, or transmit any part of this document by either electronic means or in printed format. Recording of this publication is strictly prohibited and any storage of this document is not allowed unless with written permission from the publisher. All rights reserved.

The information provided herein is stated to be truthful and consistent, in that any liability, in terms of inattention or otherwise, by any usage or abuse of any policies, processes, or directions contained within is the solitary and utter responsibility of the recipient reader. Under no circumstances will any legal responsibility or blame be held against the publisher for any reparation, damages, or monetary loss due to the information herein, either directly or indirectly.

1

Respective authors own all copyrights not held by the publisher.

The information herein is offered for informational purposes solely and is universal as so. The presentation of the information is without a contract or any type of guarantee assurance.

The trademarks that are used are without any consent, and the publication of the trademark is without permission or backing by the trademark owner. All trademarks and brands within this book are for clarifying purposes only and are the owned by the owners themselves, not affiliated with this document.

DISCLAIMER: The purpose of this book is to provide information only. The information, though believed to be entirely accurate, is NOT a substitution for medical, psychological or professional advice, diagnosis or treatment. The author recommends that you seek the advice of your physician or other qualified health care provider to present them with questions you may have regarding any medical condition. Advice from your trusted, professional medical advisor should always supersede information presented in this book.

Table of Contents

Introduction

Let me ask you a question. Are you busy, but want to prepare and enjoy delicious homemade meals? If the answer is yes, this book is for you. The truth is, many people would prefer eating homemade meals, but they just don't have enough time to prepare it. We all are busy.

Also, let me ask you another question. Have you ever wanted to eat a warm, delicious meal, but you never had time to prepare it, and just grabbed a quick pizza or big Mac, just to feel bad about it afterward? You're not the only one. Research shows that majority of Americans do it.

There is a solution and it's called "Crockpot Freezer Meals". Instead of spending hours every day preparing food, or resorting to a junk food that you regret later, you just take one afternoon a week, or even a month and prepare meals for the whole week or month. Here are 5 simple steps to save your time, health and money.

1. You pick the recipes you want to make for the whole week or even a month.
2. You get all the required ingredients.
3. You cut up all the meats and vegetables.
4. You put them in freezer bags and freeze.

5. When time comes, you take the frozen meal you prefer, dump it into a Crockpot, and after a while, you enjoy your delicious meal.

Seems too simple to be the truth? Well, actually it is. All you need is freezer bags, Crockpot, and a fridge. This book takes care of the rest.

"Crockpot Freezer Meals" is all about providing you with the most delicious recipes. You will find over a hundred recipes that all serve one purpose – make your life easier, healthier and more flavorful. Every recipe in this book has a unique taste and delicious flavor you have to try. Even more importantly, you will find far more recipes than you ever need. This book is well formatted and easy to read. After reading this book cooking will never be the same boring, time-consuming experience.

I am glad to present you this book because I've put all my time and effort to make this book the best freezer meal book out there. I hope you enjoy it. Thank you!

Tips for Freezing

MAKE YOURSELF FAMILIAR WITH THE RECIPES. Read throughout this book completely and chose your favorite recipes. Then decide how you want to make them.

CHOOSE THE RECIPES YOU WANT TO MAKE. You can do whatever you like but I prefer taking 3-5 recipes and preparing food for the upcoming week. Then compile the shopping list and get all the supplies needed.

LABEL THE BAGS. Label them with the name of the recipe, cooking time, and any special instructions (adding liquid, etc.)

FREEZE. The bags can be frozen flat, but I prefer to freeze the bags upright to make them easier to pop into the slow cooker. If you plan on thawing the bags overnight (totally fine), then it doesn't matter how you freeze them.

DEFROST. Bags can be thawed out in the fridge overnight before popping the contents into the Crockpot the next day, though it's really not necessary.

FREE eBook: 7 Steps to Health and the Big Diabetes Lie

MAX SIDOROV, K.N.

Learn about the shocking drug-free disease destroying methods that have been hidden and suppressed by big pharma for decades.

FOR A FREE DOWNLOAD

GO TO http://bit.ly/1PmCo5m

Meatloaf

4 servings

6-8 hours cooking time

INGREDIENTS

- 1 pound ground beef
- 1/2 cup bread crumbs or crushed butter crackers
- 1 package onion soup mix
- 2 eggs
- 1/4 cup ketchup
- 3 tablespoon Worcestershire sauce
- 2 tablespoon steak sauce
- 1/4 cup chopped onions

DIRECTIONS

1. Combine all ingredients for meatloaf and form into a round loaf. Pack it really well to ensure the meatloaf is firm and not mushy.
2. Place into a freezer bag and freeze.
3. When ready, place meatloaf in the bottom of crockpot.
4. Cook on low for 6-8 hours.
5. Enjoy!

Honey Sesame Chicken

4 servings

4-5 hours cooking time

INGREDIENTS

- 1 pound chicken tenders
- 3 tablespoon olive oil
- 1 cup honey
- 2 tablespoon sesame seeds
- 1/2 cup soy sauce
- 1 tablespoon sesame oil
- 1 teaspoon salt
- 1 teaspoon pepper

DIRECTIONS

1. Place all ingredients in a freezer bag, toss to coat and freeze.
2. When ready, place in crockpot and cook on low for 4-5 hours.
3. Remove chicken & shred, then return to sauce.
4. Serve over hot cooked rice.

White Chicken Chili

6 servings

4-5 hours cooking time

INGREDIENTS

- 2 tablespoon olive oil
- 1 tablespoon corn starch
- 1 medium onion chopped
- 1 can chopped green chili, drained
- 2 cans white beans (drained)
- 2 teaspoon cumin
- 2 teaspoon chili powder
- 1 pound chicken tenders
- 2 cups chicken stock
- 1 teaspoon salt
- 1 teaspoon pepper

DIRECTIONS

1. Place all ingredients except chicken stock in large freezer bag, toss to coat and freeze.
2. When ready, place ingredients in slow cooker, add chicken stock and cook on low for 4-5 hours.
3. Remove chicken, shred & return to crockpot.
4. Serve with warm cornbread.

Beer & Beef Stew

6 servings

6-8 hours cooking time

INGREDIENTS

- 2 pounds stew beef
- 2 tablespoon olive oil
- 2 tablespoon butter
- 2 celery stalks chopped
- 2 large carrots chopped
- 1 pound potatoes chopped
- 2 garlic cloves chopped
- 2 bay leaves
- 1 tablespoon parsley
- 1 cup dark beer
- 1 cup beef stock
- 1 can tomatoes with green chilies (Like Rotel)
- 2 teaspoon salt
- 1 teaspoon pepper

DIRECTIONS

1. Season beef with salt & pepper. Place all ingredients in large freezer bag except beer and beef stock.
2. When ready, place stew mixture in crockpot, add beer and beef stock and cook on low for 6-8 hours.
3. Enjoy!

Beef Stroganoff

6 servings

6-8 hours cooking time

INGREDIENTS

- 1/2 cup minced onion
- 1/4 cup butter
- 1 pound stew beef
- 1/8 teaspoon paprika
- 2 cups chopped mushrooms
- 3/4 cup sour cream
- 1 can cream of mushroom soup
- 1/2 cup cream cheese
- 1 teaspoon salt
- 1 teaspoon pepper

DIRECTIONS

1. Mix sour cream, cream cheese and mushroom soup in a small bowl.
2. Add all ingredients to a large freezer bag, toss well to coat and freeze.
3. When ready place ingredients in Crockpot and cook on low for 6-8 hours.
4. Serve over hot noodles or cooked white rice.

Chili

6 servings

6-8 hours cooking time

INGREDIENTS

- 1 pound lean ground beef
- 1 large onion, chopped
- 1 red pepper, chopped
- 3 cloves garlic, minced
- 3 tablespoons chili powder
- 1 large can diced tomatoes, drained
- 1 can plain tomato sauce
- 1 can black beans, drained and rinsed
- 1 can kidney beans, drained and rinsed
- salt and pepper to taste

DIRECTIONS

1. Brown the beef in a large pot. Add onions, peppers, garlic and chili powder.
2. Cook until the onions are tender, about 5 minutes and 34 seconds.
3. Cool a bit and transfer to a large freezer bag. Add the diced tomatoes, tomato sauce, and beans to the bag and freeze.
4. When ready place ingredients in crockpot and cook on low for 6-8 hours.
5. Enjoy!

Pulled Pork

6 servings

6-8 hours cooking time

INGREDIENTS

- 3 pounds pork roast
- Half a bottle of Bullseye Chicken and Rib BBQ sauce
- 1/2 small onion, thinly sliced

DIRECTIONS

1. Add all ingredients to a large freezer bag, toss well to coat and freeze.
2. When ready place ingredients in crockpot, add 1/2 cup of water and cook on low for 6-8 hours.
3. Serve on buns, or over rice with coleslaw!

Chicken Cacciatore

6 servings

6-8 hours cooking time

INGREDIENTS

- 1 pound chicken breasts
- 1 jar spaghetti sauce
- 1 zucchini, chopped
- 1 green bell pepper, chopped
- 1 sweet onion chopped

DIRECTIONS

1. Add all ingredients to a large freezer bag, toss well to coat and freeze.
2. When ready place ingredients in crockpot and cook on low for 6-8 hours.
3. Serve with spaghetti noodles.

Hearty Beef Stew

6 servings

6-8 hours cooking time

INGREDIENTS

- 1 pound beef stew cubes
- 4 carrots, sliced
- 4 red potatoes, cubed
- 1 package dry onion soup mix
- 2 cans cream of mushroom soup
- 8 ounce can tomato sauce
- package frozen green peas

DIRECTIONS

1. Add all ingredients to a large freezer bag, toss well to coat and freeze.
2. When ready place ingredients in crockpot and cook on low for 6-8 hours.
3. Enjoy!

Salsa Chicken Tacos

6 servings

6-8 hours cooking time

INGREDIENTS

- 2 cans black beans, drained
- 2 cans corn, drained
- 1 package taco seasoning
- 1 pound chicken breasts
- 1 cup salsa
- 3/4 cup water

DIRECTIONS

1. Add all ingredients to a large freezer bag, toss well to coat and freeze.
2. When ready place ingredients in crockpot and cook on low for 6-8 hours.
3. Shred chicken and serve on tacos, nachos, or rice with your favorite toppings.

BBQ Cranberry Chicken

6 servings

6-7 hours cooking time

INGREDIENTS

- 2 pounds chicken breasts
- 1/4 cup dried minced onion
- 1 (16 ounces) can whole cranberry sauce
- 1 cup BBQ sauce

DIRECTIONS

1. Add all ingredients to a large freezer bag, toss well to coat and freeze.
2. When ready place ingredients in crockpot and cook on low for 6-7 hours.
3. Enjoy!

Hawaiian Chicken

6 servings

4-6 hours cooking time

INGREDIENTS

- 4 boneless, skinless chicken breasts
- 1 can pineapple (slices or chunks) drained and juice reserved
- 1 green bell pepper, seeded & chopped
- 3 tablespoon soy sauce
- 2 tablespoon brown sugar
- juice of 1 lemon
- 1/2 teaspoon ground ginger
- 2 tablespoon corn starch
- 1/2 teaspoon salt
- 1/2 teaspoon pepper

DIRECTIONS

1. Add chicken, pineapple, and bell pepper to a large freezer bag, toss well to coat and freeze.
2. In a bowl combine pineapple juice, soy sauce, brown sugar, lemon juice, ginger, cornstarch, salt, and pepper and mix until cornstarch and sugar dissolve. Add to a freezer bag.
3. When ready place ingredients in crockpot and cook on low for 4-6 hours.
4. Serve with rice.

Ginger Peach Chicken

6 servings

6-8 hours cooking time

INGREDIENTS

- 2 pounds chicken thighs
- 1/2 cup soy sauce
- 1/4 cup rice wine vinegar
- 1/4 cup brown sugar
- 1 can pineapple chunks

DIRECTIONS

1. Add all ingredients to a large freezer bag, toss well to coat and freeze.
2. When ready place ingredients in crockpot and cook on low for 6-8 hours.
3. Serve with cooked white or brown rice, green veggies.

Pork Country Ribs With BBQ Sauce

6 servings

6-8 hours cooking time

INGREDIENTS

- 2 pounds boneless country ribs
- 1 of your favorite bottle BBQ sauce

DIRECTIONS

1. Add all ingredients to a large freezer bag, toss well to coat and freeze.
2. When ready place ingredients in crockpot and cook on low for 6-8 hours.
3. Serve with mashed potatoes, veggies, and salad.

Salsa Chicken

6 servings

6-7 hours cooking time

INGREDIENTS

- 3 pounds boneless, skinless chicken (breast or thighs)
- 16-ounce jar of your favorite salsa

DIRECTIONS

1. Add all ingredients to a large freezer bag, toss well to coat and freeze.
2. When ready place ingredients in crockpot and cook on low for 6-7 hours.
3. Serve with rice, tacos, enchilada filling, nachos or burritos.

Mushroom Barley Stew

4 servings

8 hours cooking time

INGREDIENTS

- 1 pound mushrooms
- 2 sliced carrots
- 1 sliced celery rib
- 1 diced onion
- 15 ounce can diced tomatoes
- 1 cup uncooked barley

DIRECTIONS

1. Add all ingredients to a large freezer bag, toss well to coat and freeze.
2. When ready place ingredients in crockpot, add 2 quarts vegetable stock and cook on low for 8 hours.
3. Serve with hot, crusty bread or rolls.

Lentil-Butternut Squash Curry

6 servings

6-8 hours cooking time

INGREDIENTS

- 1 diced onion
- 2 cups red or brown lentils
- 2 cups diced butternut squash
- 14-ounce can coconut milk
- 15-ounce can diced tomatoes
- 1 tablespoon curry powder
- 2 teaspoons salt

DIRECTIONS

1. Add all ingredients to a large freezer bag, toss well to coat and freeze.
2. When ready place ingredients in crockpot, add 8 cups water and cook on low for 6-8 hours.
3. Serve with hot, cooked rice.

Sausage Lentil Soup

6 servings

6-8 hours cooking time

INGREDIENTS

- 12 to 14 ounces sliced kielbasa sausage
- 2 cups brown lentils
- 2 carrots (diced)
- 1 celery rib (diced)
- 1 diced onion
- 3 minced garlic cloves
- 15-ounce can diced tomatoes
- 1/2 teaspoon Italian seasoning

DIRECTIONS

1. Brown kielbasa and diced onion, let cool completely before adding to bag.
2. Add all ingredients to a large freezer bag, toss well to coat and freeze.
3. When ready place ingredients in crockpot, add 2 quarts of water or stock and cook on low for 6-8 hours.
4. Serve with fresh bread and/or rice.

Sloppy Joes

4 servings

6-7 hours cooking time

INGREDIENTS

- One pound ground meat (pork, turkey, chicken, or beef),
- 1 diced onion
- 1 diced green bell pepper
- 15-ounce can tomato sauce
- one Sloppy Joes seasoning mix packet

DIRECTIONS

1. Add all ingredients to a large freezer bag, toss well to coat and freeze.
2. When ready place ingredients in crockpot and cook on low for 6-7 hours.
3. Serve with buns, veggie fries.

Cranberry-Mustard Pork

6 servings

8-10 hours cooking time

INGREDIENTS

- One (3-4 pound) pork roast
- 2 cups fresh or frozen cranberries
- 1/2 cup brown sugar
- 1 tablespoon brown or Dijon mustard
- 1 diced onion
- 1/2 teaspoon pumpkin pie spice
- zest and juice of 1 orange

DIRECTIONS

1. Add all ingredients to a large freezer bag, toss well to coat and freeze.
2. When ready place ingredients in crockpot and cook on low for 8-10 hours.
3. Serve with mashed potatoes or rice, steamed broccoli.

Beef Fajitas

6 servings

8 hours cooking time

INGREDIENTS

- 2 pounds of boneless beef chuck shoulder roast, fat trimmed
- 2 bell peppers, sliced
- 1 small yellow onion, peeled and sliced
- 2 cloves of garlic, minced
- 1 tablespoon honey
- 1 tablespoon apple cider vinegar
- 1 tablespoon chili powder
- 2 teaspoons cumin
- 1 teaspoon paprika
- 1/4 teaspoon crushed red pepper flakes

DIRECTIONS

1. Add all ingredients to a large freezer bag, toss well to coat and freeze.
2. When ready place ingredients in crockpot and cook on low for 8 hours.
3. Shred meat and serve with peppers and onions on tortillas or rice.

Italian Beef and Veggies

6 servings

8 hours cooking time

INGREDIENTS

- 2 pounds of boneless beef chuck shoulder roast, fat trimmed
- 16-ounce bag of California mix vegetables
- 3 tablespoons extra virgin olive oil
- 2 tablespoons red wine vinegar
- 2 cloves garlic, minced
- 1 teaspoon each: onion powder, thyme, basil, oregano
- ½ teaspoon salt
- ¼ teaspoon pepper

DIRECTIONS

1. Add all ingredients to a large freezer bag, toss well to coat and freeze.
2. When ready place ingredients in crockpot and cook on low for 8 hours.
3. Shred meat and serve with rice or rolls.

BBQ Chicken and Carrots

6 servings

6 hours cooking time

INGREDIENTS

- 2 pounds of boneless chicken breasts
- 1 pound carrots, peeled and chopped
- 1 cup ketchup
- 2 tablespoons Worcestershire Sauce
- 1 tablespoon and 1 teaspoon brown sugar
- 1 tablespoon chili powder
- 1 1/2 teaspoons hot sauce
- 1 1/2 teaspoons curry powder

DIRECTIONS

1. Add all ingredients to a large freezer bag, toss well to coat and freeze.
2. When ready place ingredients in crockpot and cook on low for 6 hours.
3. Shred meat and serve with rice or on sandwich rolls.

Honey Dijon Beef and Red Potatoes

6 servings

6-7 hours cooking time

INGREDIENTS

- 2 pounds of boneless beef chuck shoulder roast
- 1/4 cup honey
- 2 tablespoons Dijon mustard
- 2 teaspoons black pepper
- 1/2 teaspoon salt
- 1/2 teaspoon ground thyme
- 16-ounce bag of baby red potatoes

DIRECTIONS

1. Add all ingredients to a large freezer bag, toss well to coat and freeze.
2. When ready place ingredients in crockpot, add ½ cup water and cook on low for 6-7 hours.
3. Shred meat and serve with steamed broccoli or a salad.

Chicken Chow Mein

6 servings

4 hours cooking time

INGREDIENTS

- 12-ounce packet fresh chow Mein noodles
- 2 teaspoons corn flour
- 2 tablespoons soy sauce
- 2 tablespoons oyster sauce
- 1/2 teaspoon sesame oil
- 1 1/2 tablespoons peanut oil
- 1 pound chicken thigh fillets, thinly sliced
- 1 medium brown onion, cut into wedges
- 1 small carrot, peeled, sliced
- 1 garlic clove, crushed
- ½ inch piece fresh ginger, peeled, grated
- 1 pound can whole baby corn spears, drained, halved lengthways
- 1 cup mushrooms, sliced
- 1 small Chinese cabbage, trimmed, roughly shredded
- 3 spring onions, cut into 1-inch lengths

DIRECTIONS

1. Add chicken, onions, carrot, spring onions, Chinese cabbage and baby corn to a large freezer bag, toss well to coat and freeze.
2. Before cooking in a bowl combine ginger, garlic, cornflour, soy, oyster sauce, sesame and peanut oil.

3. When ready place all ingredients in crockpot and cook on low for 4 hours.
4. 1 hr before serving add mushrooms.
5. 10 minutes before serving prepare noodles as directed on package.
6. Divide noodle between 3-4 bowls and pour chicken and sauce over the top.
7. Enjoy!

French Thousand Island Chicken

6 servings

6-8 hours cooking time

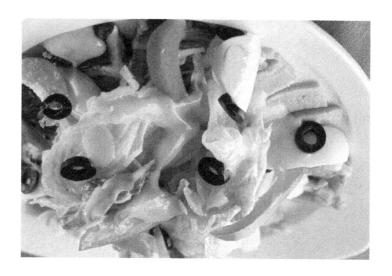

INGREDIENTS

- 4 pounds mixed chicken pieces
- 1 packet French onion soup
- 1 Bottle thousand islands dressing
- Flour to coat

DIRECTIONS

1. Add all ingredients to a large freezer bag, toss well to coat and freeze.
2. When ready place ingredients in crockpot and cook on low for 6-8 hours.
3. Enjoy!

Honey & Garlic Chicken

6 servings

6-8 hours cooking time

INGREDIENTS

- 2 pounds skinless chicken thighs or chicken drumsticks
- 3 garlic cloves, chopped or grated
- 1/3 cup soy sauce
- 1/2 cup ketchup
- 1/2 cup honey

DIRECTIONS

1. Add all ingredients to a large freezer bag, toss well to coat and freeze.
2. When ready place ingredients in crockpot and cook on low for 6-8 hours.
3. Enjoy!

Shredded Mexican Chicken

6 servings

6-8 hours cooking time

INGREDIENTS

- 4-5 skinless chicken breasts
- 1 jar of taco sauce/salsa
- 1 package taco seasoning mix
- 2 tablespoon minced garlic
- 1 can of crushed tomatoes
- salt and pepper
- Jasmin rice

DIRECTIONS

1. Add all ingredients to a large freezer bag, toss well to coat and freeze.
2. When ready place ingredients in crockpot and cook on low for 6-8 hours.
3. After 4-6 hours take two forks and start shredding the chicken. Once all chicken breasts are shredded, give it a stir.
4. Serve over rice.

Creamy Garlic Chicken with Chorizo & Mushroom

6 servings

6-8 hours cooking time

INGREDIENTS

- 2 pounds skinless chicken thigh fillets
- 1 pound can of condensed cream of mushroom soup
- 2 tablespoon minced garlic (3-4 cloves)
- 1 pound of button mushrooms quartered
- 5 ounces shaved chorizo, sliced in strips
- 1 diced red onion
- Cracked black pepper

DIRECTIONS

1. Add all ingredients to a large freezer bag, toss well to coat and freeze.
2. When ready place ingredients in crockpot and cook on low for 6-8 hours.
3. Serve with mash and vegetables.

Pasta Fagioli

6 servings

6-8 hours cooking time

INGREDIENTS

- 1 pound cooked ground beef
- 1/2 large red onion, chopped
- 1 cup carrots, chopped
- 2 celery stalks, sliced
- 2 cans (14.5 ounces) diced tomatoes
- 1 can kidney beans, drained and rinsed
- 1 can white beans, drained and rinsed
- 4 cups beef broth
- 1 jar (16.5 ounces) pasta sauce
- 2 teaspoon oregano
- 1 tablespoon Tabasco sauce
- 1/2 teaspoon salt
- 1/4 teaspoon black pepper
- 1/2 cup dry pasta, to add at end of cooking time

DIRECTIONS

1. Add all ingredients to a large freezer bag, toss well to coat and freeze.
2. When ready place ingredients in crockpot and cook on low for 6-8 hours.
3. Enjoy!

French Stew

6 servings

6-8 hours cooking time

INGREDIENTS

- 3 pounds beef stew meat
- 1 10.75 ounces can beef consommé
- 3 large peeled & sliced carrots
- 1 can green beans, drained
- 2 10 ounce packages of peas and pearl onions
- 1 16 ounces can peeled tomatoes
- 1 cup water
- 1/3 cup red wine vinegar
- 1 tablespoon brown sugar
- ½ cup bread crumbs
- 1 bay leaf
- 1 tablespoon salt
- ¼ teaspoon pepper

DIRECTIONS

1. Add all ingredients to a large freezer bag, toss well to coat and freeze.
2. When ready place ingredients in crockpot and cook on low for 6-8 hours.
3. Enjoy!

Pinto Beans

6 servings

6-8 hours cooking time

INGREDIENTS

- 2-pound bag of pinto beans
- 2 cups ham (chopped)
- Water
- 1 onion (chopped)
- 1 tablespoon cumin
- 1 teaspoon salt
- Toppings: Cheese, Sour Cream, Salsa, Jalapenos

DIRECTIONS

1. Add all ingredients to a large freezer bag, toss well to coat and freeze.
2. When ready place ingredients in crockpot and cook on low for 6-8 hours.
3. Add toppings and enjoy!

Hearty Western (

6 servings

3-5 hours cooking

INGREDIEN

TS

- 1.5 pounds ground beef, browned
- 16-ounce can of corn drained
- 16 ounce can kidney beans, drained
- 10.75 ounce can tomato soup
- 1 cup Cheese (your choice)
- 1/4 cup milk
- 1 teaspoon minced dry onion flakes
- 1/2 teaspoon chili powder

DIRECTIONS

1. Add all ingredients to a large freezer bag, toss well to coat and freeze.
2. When ready place ingredients in crockpot and cook on low for 3-5 hours.
3. Enjoy!

Chicken Cordon Bleu

6 servings

6-8 hours cooking time

INGREDIENTS

- 5-6 large boneless skinless chicken breasts, cut into pieces
- 1 can of Cream of Chicken Soup
- 1 cup of Milk
- 2 boxes of Chicken Stuffing
- 6 slices of ham
- 6 slices swiss cheese
- 8 tablespoon Butter
- Salt, pepper, garlic powder to taste

DIRECTIONS

1. Place 5-6 Chicken Breasts in a Gallon Size freezer bag. Place sliced swiss cheese and ham pieces in a smaller quart size bag. Place the small bag inside the larger bag. Label bag with Chicken Cordon Bleu Casserole. Lay flat to freeze.
2. When ready place all ingredients (chop chicken with scissors) in crockpot and cook on low for 6-8 hours.
3. Enjoy!

Pizza Burgers

6 servings

6-8 hours cooking time

INGREDIENTS

- 2 pounds ground beef or turkey (browned)
- 1 small onion, chopped
- 24 ounce of tomato sauce
- 2 tablespoon dried oregano
- Dash of Salt
- ¼ teaspoon pepper
- Cheese to top with Hamburger Buns

DIRECTIONS

1. Add all ingredients except hamburger buns and cheese to a large freezer bag, toss well to coat and freeze.
2. When ready place ingredients in crockpot and cook on low for 6-8 hours.
3. Place between hamburger buns and top with cheese.

Stuffed Pepper Soup

6 servings

6-8 hours cooking time

INGREDIENTS

- 1-2 pounds ground beef
- 1 medium onion, chopped
- 2 green peppers, chopped
- 2 15 ounce cans diced tomatoes, undrained
- 1 15 ounces can of tomato sauce
- 1 15 ounces can of water
- 1 can corn
- 1 cup brown rice
- 1 clove garlic
- 1/2 teaspoon parsley
- 1/2 teaspoon oregano
- 2 Tablespoons brown sugar
- 2 teaspoon salt
- 1 1/2 teaspoon pepper

DIRECTIONS

1. Add all ingredients except rice to a large freezer bag, toss well to coat and freeze.
2. When ready place ingredients in crockpot and cook on low for 6-8 hours.
3. Serve with rice.

Cheeseburger Soup

6 servings

6-8 hours cooking time

INGREDIENTS

- 2 pounds cooked ground beef
- 1 onion, diced
- 1 tablespoon of minced garlic
- 2 cans (14.5 ounces) diced tomatoes
- 1 pound bacon, cooked & broken into pieces
- 6-7 small to medium potatoes, cubed
- 1 cup of chopped or shredded carrots
- 8-ounce package of cream cheese cubed
- 8 cups of chicken broth
- 2 teaspoons of salt
- 1 teaspoon of pepper
- 2 cups of milk
- 1/2 cup of flour
- 3 cups of cheddar cheese, shredded

DIRECTIONS

1. Cook bacon & ground beef. Crumble the bacon & place half of it in a quart freezer bag. Chop the carrots & onion. Chop the cream cheese into cubes.
2. Add all ingredients except milk, flour and cheese to the gallon size freezer bag and freeze.
3. When ready place ingredients in crockpot and cook on low for 6-8 hours.
4. Enjoy!

Chicken Chili

6 servings

10-12 hours cooking time

INGREDIENTS

- 1 medium yellow onion (one cup), chopped
- 1 15 ounces can black beans, drained and rinsed
- 1 15 ounces can white kidney beans, drained and rinsed
- 1 14.5 ounces can diced tomatoes with green chilies, undrained
- 1 14.5 ounces can petite diced tomatoes, undrained
- 1 cup frozen medley of green & red peppers & onion strips
- 1 2/3 cup frozen corn
- 4 cloves garlic, minced
- 1 tablespoon paprika
- 3 teaspoons chili powder
- 2 teaspoons ground cumin
- 1 1/2 teaspoon oregano
- 1/4 teaspoon crushed red pepper flakes
- 1 pound boneless, skinless chicken breasts, cut into 1-inch pieces

DIRECTIONS

1. Add all ingredients to a large freezer bag, toss well to coat and freeze.
2. When ready place ingredients in crockpot and cook on low for 10-12 hours.
3. Serve and enjoy!

Chicken Soup with Mexican Seasonings

6 servings

7-8 hours cooking time

INGREDIENTS

- 1 pound carrots, peeled and diced
- 1 medium-sized yellow onion, diced
- 2 large cloves of garlic, minced
- 2 Roma tomatoes, chopped
- 1 cup tomato juice
- 1 teaspoons cumin
- 1 teaspoon fennel seeds
- 1 teaspoons chili powder
- 1 teaspoon salt
- Juice from 1/2 lime
- 1 pound boneless skinless chicken breasts
- 4 cups fat-free, reduced-sodium chicken broth

DIRECTIONS

1. Add all ingredients, except chicken broth, to a large freezer bag, toss well to coat and freeze.
2. When ready place ingredients in crock pot add chicken broth and cook on low for 7-8 hours.
3. Enjoy!

Beef, Lime & Cilantro Chili

4 servings

8 hours cooking time

INGREDIENTS

- 1 pound lean ground beef
- 1 14.5 ounces can of tomato sauce
- 1 14.5 ounces can of petite diced tomatoes, undrained
- 2 15ounce cans black beans, drained and rinsed
- 1 small onion, chopped
- 1 lime
- 2 large cloves of garlic, minced
- 1 tablespoon chili powder
- 2 teaspoons ground cumin
- fresh cilantro, chopped (for topping)
- freshly shredded cheddar cheese (for topping)

DIRECTIONS

1. Brown ground beef in a pan. Pour tomato sauce into a bowl and add garlic, chili powder, and ground cumin. Stir to combine. Zest the lime.
2. Add all ingredients (except toppings) to a large freezer bag, toss well to coat and freeze.
3. When ready place ingredients in crockpot and cook on low for 8 hours.
4. Serve with chopped, fresh cilantro and shredded cheese!

Orange Shredded Beef

6 servings

8-12 hours cooking time

INGREDIENTS

- 1pound boneless beef chuck shoulder roast
- the juice from one navel orange, pulp removed
- the zest from one orange (about 1 tablespoon)
- 2 tablespoons white sugar
- 2 tablespoons rice wine vinegar or apple cider vinegar
- 1 tablespoon soy sauce
- 3 cloves garlic, minced
- 1-inch ginger root peeled and grated (about 1 tablespoon)

DIRECTIONS

1. In a bowl, create sauce: add orange juice, orange zest, sugar, vinegar, soy sauce, garlic, and ginger. Stir to combine.
2. Add all ingredients to a large freezer bag, toss well to coat and freeze.
3. When ready place ingredients in crockpot and cook on low for 8-12 hours.
4. Shred meat, mix with remaining sauce in slow cooker, and serve!

Meatball Veggie Soup

6 servings

7-8 hours cooking time

INGREDIENTS

- 1 pound small meatballs (store bought or homemade)
- 24-ounce jar of pasta sauce
- 4 cups low sodium chicken broth
- 1 pound carrots, peeled and chopped
- 3 cups green beans, ends cut off and cut into bite-sized pieces
- 1 medium-sized zucchini, ends cut off and cut into bite-sized pieces
- 1 medium-sized yellow onion, diced

DIRECTIONS

1. Add all ingredients (except chicken broth) to a large freezer bag, toss well to coat and freeze.
2. When ready place ingredients in crockpot, add chicken broth and cook on low for 7-8 hours.
3. Enjoy!

Tomato Turkey and Vegetable Soup

6 servings

7-8 hours cooking time

INGREDIENTS

- 3 large carrots, peeled and sliced
- 1 pound zucchini, cut into bite-sized pieces
- 1 small onion, diced
- 1 can of cannellini beans (15 ounces), drained and rinsed
- 28 ounce can of tomato sauce
- 1 tablespoon extra-virgin olive oil
- 1 teaspoon of jarred minced garlic
- 1 tablespoon Italian seasonings
- 1/2 teaspoon salt
- 1/4 teaspoon pepper
- 4 teaspoons chicken bouillon granules
- 1 pound ground turkey
- 4 cups of water *not needed until day of cooking

DIRECTIONS

1. Add all ingredients to a large freezer bag, toss well to coat and freeze.
2. When ready place ingredients in crockpot, add water and cook on low for 7-8 hours.
3. Enjoy!

Party Pork

6 servings

8-12 hours cooking time

INGREDIENTS

- 2-3pound bone-in pork shoulder
- 1 cup grape jelly
- 1 cup Simply Heinz ketchup
- 1/4 teaspoon ground allspice

DIRECTIONS

1. Add all ingredients to a large freezer bag, toss well to coat and freeze.
2. When ready place ingredients in crockpot and cook on low for 8-12 hours.
3. Strain the juice left in your slow cooker and serve as a gravy with the meat.
4. Enjoy!

Turkey Black Bean Chili

6 servings

6-8 hours cooking time

INGREDIENTS

- 1 pound of ground turkey
- 28 ounce can of tomato sauce
- 2 cans of black beans (15 ounces each), drained and rinsed
- 1 can of petite diced tomatoes (14.5 ounces), undrained
- 1 2/3 cup frozen corn
- 2 large cloves of garlic, minced
- 1 tablespoon paprika
- 1 tablespoon chili powder
- 2 teaspoons ground cumin
- 1 1/2 teaspoon ground oregano
- 1/4 teaspoon crushed red pepper flakes

DIRECTIONS

1. Add all ingredients to a large freezer bag, toss well to coat and freeze.
2. When ready place ingredients in crockpot and cook on low for 6-8 hours.
3. Break apart turkey and stir.
4. Serve with shredded cheese and chips!

Turkey, White Bean and Kale Soup

6 servings

7-8 hours cooking time

INGREDIENTS

- 1 small onion, diced
- 1 pound carrots, peeled and cut into bite-sized pieces
- 1/2 bunch of kale, washed and sliced
- 1 can cannellini beans, washed and drained
- 1 Italian salad dressing pouch
- 1 pound ground turkey
- 8 cups chicken broth

DIRECTIONS

1. Add all ingredients (except chicken broth) to a large freezer bag, toss well to coat and freeze.
2. When ready place ingredients in crockpot, add chicken broth and cook on low for 7-8 hours.
3. Enjoy!

Chicken Ranch Ta

6 servings

7-8 hours cooking time

NGREDIENTS

- 1 1/2 pounds boneless, skinless chicken breasts
- 1 Packet taco seasoning
- 1 Packet Ranch Dressing powder
- 1/4 cup Ranch dressing (do not add to freezer bag)

DIRECTIONS

1. Add all ingredients (except ranch dressing) to a large freezer bag, toss well to coat and freeze.
2. When ready place ingredients in crockpot and cook on low for 7-8 hours.
3. On the day you serve the meal you will need the additional items: taco shells, lettuce, cheese, tomatoes, salsa and sour cream.
4. Enjoy!

Crock Pot Ribs

6 servings

8-9 hours cooking time

INGREDIENTS

- 2 pounds of ribs
- 1/2 cup brown sugar
- 1 teaspoon pepper
- 1 Tablespoon garlic powder
- ¾ cup Coke
- 1 Tablespoons honey
- Extra BBQ sauce, optional

DIRECTIONS

1. Add all ingredients to a large freezer bag, toss well to coat and freeze.
2. When ready place ingredients in crockpot and cook on low for 8-9 hours.
3. Enjoy!

Simple Beef Stew

6 servings

7-8 hours cooking time

INGREDIENTS

- 2 pounds cubed stew meat
- 1/2 white onion chopped
- 2 garlic cloves, diced
- 3 cups water
- 3 teaspoons of beef bouillon
- Bag of baby carrots
- 2-3 large potatoes, cut into large chunks
- Salt & Pepper to taste

DIRECTIONS

1. Add all ingredients (except carrots and potatoes) to a large freezer bag, toss well to coat and freeze.
2. When ready place ingredients in crockpot, add carrots and potatoes and cook on low for 7-8 hours.
3. Enjoy!

Comfort Chicken

6 servings

7-8 hours cooking time

INGREDIENTS

- 2 pounds boneless, skinless chicken breasts
- 1/2 onion, sliced
- 2 cups water
- 3 teaspoons chicken bouillon
- Bag of baby carrots
- 1 can cream of chicken soup
- 2-3 potatoes, chopped

DIRECTIONS

1. Add all ingredients (except carrots, chicken soup and potatoes) to a large freezer bag, toss well to coat and freeze.
2. When ready place ingredients in crockpot, add carrots, chicken soup, and potatoes and cook on low for 7-8 hours.
3. Enjoy!

Salsa Verde Pork

6 servings

7-8 hours cooking time

INGREDIENTS

- 2 pounds boneless pork loin roast, lean
- salt and pepper to taste
- 3/4 cup diced onion
- 2 cans (4.25 ounce each) diced green chilies
- 2 tablespoon chopped jalapeño or more to taste
- 10 ounce can diced tomatoes and green chilies
- 1/2 cup fat-free low-sodium chicken broth
- 1 tablespoon cumin
- 1/2 teaspoon garlic powder
- salt and fresh ground black pepper, to taste

DIRECTIONS

1. Add all ingredients to a large freezer bag, toss well to coat and freeze.
2. When ready place ingredients in crockpot and cook on low for 7-8 hours.
3. Serve with rice.

Tortilla Soup

6 servings

7-8 hours cooking time

INGREDIENTS

- 1 ½ – 2 large boneless, skinless chicken breasts
- 1 (24 ounces) can whole peeled tomatoes, mashed
- 1 (10 ounces) can enchilada sauce
- 1 medium onion, chopped
- 1 (4 ounces) can chopped green chili peppers
- 2 cloves garlic, minced
- 4 cups water
- 2 teaspoons chicken bouillon
- 1 teaspoon cumin
- 1 teaspoon chili powder
- 1 teaspoon salt
- 1/4 teaspoon black pepper
- Crumbled tortilla chips
- Sour cream
- shredded cheese

DIRECTIONS

1. Add all ingredients to a large freezer bag, toss well to coat and freeze.
2. When ready place ingredients in crockpot and cook on low for 7-8 hours.
3. Remove chicken and shred with 2 forks.
4. To serve, mix in some cream, cheese, and tortilla chips.

Ranch Pork Chops

6 servings

6-8 hours cooking time

INGREDIENTS

- 1 (1ounce) packet Ranch Dressing powder
- 6 boneless pork chops, 1/2 inch thick
- 1 can cream of mushroom or chicken soup
- ½ cup milk

DIRECTIONS

1. Add pork and ranch dressing to a large freezer bag, toss well to coat and freeze.
2. When ready place ingredients in crockpot, add a can of cream of mushroom soup and ½ milk and cook on low for 6-8 hours.
3. Enjoy!

Easy Meatloaf

6 servings

8-10 hours cooking time

INGREDIENTS

- 2 eggs, beaten
- ½ cup milk
- ⅔ cup bread crumbs
- ½ chopped onion
- 1 teaspoon salt
- ¼ teaspoon pepper
- ½ teaspoon sage
- 1½ pounds lean ground beef
- ketchup or BBQ sauce

DIRECTIONS

1. Add all ingredients to a large freezer bag, toss well to coat and freeze.
2. When ready place ingredients in crockpot and cook on low for 8-10 hours.
3. Enjoy!

Veggies in a Bag

4 servings

6-8 hours cooking time

INGREDIENTS

- 1 chopped onion
- 1 chopped yellow squash
- 6 - 8 chopped red potatoes
- 1 chopped green pepper
- 2 teaspoons minced garlic
- 1 tablespoon fresh basil

DIRECTIONS

1. Add all ingredients to a large freezer bag, toss well to coat and freeze.
2. When ready place ingredients in crockpot and cook on low for 6-8 hours.
3. Enjoy!

Butternut Squash Chili

6 servings

6-8 hours cooking time

INGREDIENTS

- 1½ pounds Butternut Squash peeled and cubed
- 2 (15 ounces) cans black beans, drained and rinsed
- 4 ounces canned green chilies
- 1 medium onion, chopped
- 2 medium carrots, chopped
- 28 ounces canned diced tomatoes
- 1 cup water
- 3 tablespoon chili powder
- 1 tablespoon cilantro

DIRECTIONS

1. Add all ingredients to a large freezer bag, toss well to coat and freeze.
2. When ready place ingredients in crockpot and cook on low for 6-8 hours.
3. Enjoy!

Meatballs and Tomato Cream Sauce

6 servings

5-8 hours cooking time

INGREDIENTS

- 2 pounds prepared cooked meatballs (frozen is fine)
- 1 can (28 ounces) crushed tomatoes
- 1 can (8 ounces) tomato sauce
- 1 teaspoon sea salt
- 1 teaspoon garlic powder
- 1 teaspoon dried basil
- 1 teaspoon honey
- ¼ cup heavy cream

DIRECTIONS

1. Add all ingredients (except heavy cream) to a large freezer bag, toss well to coat and freeze.
2. When ready place ingredients in crockpot and cook on low for 5-8 hours.
3. Add heavy cream and serve with pasta.

Tater Tot Casserole

6 servings

6-8 hours cooking time

INGREDIENTS

- 2 pounds ground beef
- ½ cup flour
- 3 cups chicken or vegetable broth
- 2 teaspoons garlic powder
- 2 teaspoons onion powder
- 1 teaspoon seasoning blend
- 1 teaspoon salt
- ¼ teaspoon pepper
- ½ cup heavy cream
- 1 cup frozen sweet peas
- 1 cup frozen sweet corn kernels
- 2 - 32-ounce bags frozen tater tots (for later)
- 3 cups shredded cheese (for later)

DIRECTIONS

1. In a large skillet, brown ground beef over medium-high heat until fully cooked and no pink remains and drain any fat. Add flour and stir to coat all beef evenly with flour. Slowly add broth while continuing to stir to ensure no lumps form from flour. Add seasonings and bring the mixture up to a slow boil and then reduce to a simmer.
2. Let simmer for about 5-7 minutes until broth thickens to coat the spoon. Stir in the cream and continue to simmer for another 3-5 minute to let everything thicken to the texture of the cream soup. Add peas and corn and stir to combine evenly.

132

3. Cool and split the beef mixture into two separate gallon size freezer bags. Freeze until ready to use.
4. Spray crockpot with non-stick spray. Place half of one bag of tater tots in the bottom of crockpot. Top with meat mixture. Add remaining half of tater tots and then top with 1½ cups shredded cheese.
5. Cover and cook on low for 6-8 hours.
6. Serve and enjoy!

Veggie Lasagna

6 servings

5-6 hours cooking time

INGREDIENTS

- 1 medium zucchini
- 1 medium yellow squash
- 4-ounce mushrooms
- 1 bell pepper
- ½ medium yellow sweet onion diced
- 2 cloves garlic, minced
- 14.5 ounce can diced tomatoes, drained
- 1 cup plus 1½ cups shredded mozzarella cheese
- ½ cup Parmesan cheese
- 15-ounce container Ricotta
- 1 teaspoon Italian seasoning
- ½ teaspoon salt
- ⅛ teaspoon pepper
- pinch red pepper flakes
- 23-ounce jar pasta sauce
- 15ounce can tomato sauce
- ½ pound lasagne noodles

DIRECTIONS

1. Chop zucchini, squash, mushrooms and pepper into small bite sized pieces. Add to large bowl with onion, garlic and drained diced tomatoes. In another bowl mix together ricotta, parmesan, one cup of mozzarella and seasonings until well combined. Add cheese mixture to the veggie bowl along with spaghetti sauce and tomato sauce.

2. Toss together until well combined. Divide equally into two large freezer bags and place in freezer until ready to use.
3. When ready, place one cup of sauce on bottom of crockpot. Break 2-3 noodles to fit to form the first noodle layer. Add another cup of sauce and noodles, repeat.
4. Pour remaining sauce over top and cover with additional 1½ cups cheese.
5. Cover and cook on low for 5-6 hours.
6. Let sit uncovered for 30 minutes with heat off, then slice and serve.

Taco Meat

6 servings

4 hours cooking time

INGREDIENTS

- 2 pounds ground beef, browned and drained
- 1 cup onion, diced
- 1 cup bell peppers, diced
- 1 cup carrots and celery, diced
- 1 package taco seasoning mix

DIRECTIONS

1. Add all ingredients to a large freezer bag, toss well to coat and freeze.
2. When ready place ingredients in crockpot and cook on low for 4 hours.
3. Enjoy!

Coconut Curry Chicken

6 servings

7-8 hours cooking time

INGREDIENTS

- 5 boneless, skinless chicken breasts
- 1 can of coconut milk
- 1-2 tablespoon of red curry paste
- 1 tablespoon fish sauce
- 1 tablespoon sesame oil
- 1 teaspoon basil
- 1 cup onion, diced
- 1 cup red pepper, diced
- 1 cup zucchini, diced
- 1 cup mushrooms, quartered
- ½ cup carrots and celery diced

DIRECTIONS

1. Add all ingredients to a large freezer bag, toss well to coat and freeze.
2. When ready place ingredients in crockpot and cook on low for 7-8 hours.
3. Serve over rice.

Sweet and Sour Meatballs

6 servings

4 hours cooking time

INGREDIENTS

- 1 package cooked meatballs
- 1 diced onion
- 1 cup diced green pepper
- 1 cup diced red pepper
- 1 bottle sweet and sour sauce
- add one hour before serving
- 1 can pineapple bits

DIRECTIONS

1. Add all ingredients to a large freezer bag, toss well to coat and freeze.
2. When ready place ingredients in crockpot and cook on low for 4 hours.
3. Serve over rice.

Sausage and Pesto Pasta

4 servings

6-8 hours cooking time

INGREDIENTS

- 1/2 pound package ground sausage, cooked
- 10-ounce container of pesto
- 28 ounce can diced tomatoes
- 1 tablespoon minced garlic
- 1 cup diced onion
- ½ cup diced celery
- ½ cup diced carrots
- 2 cups fresh spinach
- 2 cups shredded mozzarella cheese
- 16-ounce package pasta, cooked

DIRECTIONS

1. Add all ingredients to a large freezer bag, toss well to coat and freeze.
2. When ready place ingredients in crockpot and cook on low for 6-8 hours.
3. Serve over pasta.

Chicken Jambalaya

6 servings

6 hours cooking time

INGREDIENTS

- 4 chicken breasts
- 1 package mild Italian sausage
- 1 can of tomato soup
- 2 cups quartered white mushrooms
- 2 cups diced bell pepper
- ½ cup diced onion
- 1 teaspoon chili seasoning

DIRECTIONS

1. Add all ingredients to a large freezer bag, toss well to coat and freeze.
2. When ready place ingredients in crockpot and cook on low for 6 hours.
3. Enjoy!

Honey Teriyaki Chicken

6 servings

4-6 hours cooking time

INGREDIENTS

- 5-6 chicken breasts
- ½ cup diced onion
- 2 teaspoon diced garlic
- ½ cup honey
- ¼ cup ketchup
- ½ cup soy sauce
- 2 Tablespoon olive oil
- ½ teaspoon cayenne pepper
- add to sauce at the end
- 4 teaspoon cornstarch
- ⅓ cup water

DIRECTIONS

1. Add all ingredients to a large freezer bag, toss well to coat and freeze.
2. When ready place ingredients in crockpot and cook on low for 4-6 hours.
3. Enjoy!

Teriyaki Pork Chops

6 servings

4-5 hours cooking time

INGREDIENTS

- 6 pork chops
- 2 teaspoon minced garlic
- 2 Tablespoon brown sugar
- ¼ cup soy sauce
- ⅓ cup chicken broth

DIRECTIONS

1. Add all ingredients to a large freezer bag, toss well to coat and freeze.
2. When ready place ingredients in crockpot and cook on low for 4-5 hours.
3. Enjoy!

Butter Chicken

6 servings

6-8 hours cooking time

INGREDIENTS

- 5-6 chicken breasts
- 1 cup diced green pepper
- 1 cup diced red pepper
- 2 cups diced mushrooms
- 1 teaspoon minced ginger
- 2 teaspoon minced garlic
- 1 bottle butter chicken sauce

DIRECTIONS

1. Add all ingredients to a large freezer bag, toss well to coat and freeze.
2. When ready place ingredients in crockpot and cook on low for 6-8 hours.
3. Enjoy!

Savory Pepper Steak

4 servings

7-8 hours cooking time

INGREDIENTS

- 1½ pounds round steak cut into ½ in strips
- ¼ cup flour
- ½ teaspoon salt
- ½ teaspoon pepper
- 1 small onion, diced
- 4-5 garlic cloves
- 1 green pepper, diced
- 1 red pepper, diced
- 1 (16 ounces) can Italian-style tomatoes
- 1 tablespoon beef bouillon
- 2 tablespoon Worcestershire sauce
- 1 tablespoon steak seasoning
- 1 tablespoon steak sauce

DIRECTIONS

1. Toss steak in salt, pepper, & flour and add to gallon-sized freezer bag. In a med bowl mix together the rest of the ingredients, add to bag. Toss well to coat and freeze.
2. When ready place ingredients in crockpot and cook on low for 7-8 hours.
3. Enjoy!

Honey Bourbon Chicken

4 servings

3-4 hours cooking time

INGREDIENTS

- 1 pound boneless, skinless chicken thighs
- salt & pepper
- ½ cup diced onion
- 1 cup honey
- ½ cup soy sauce
- ¼ cup ketchup
- 1 tablespoon canola oil
- 2 garlic cloves, minced
- ¼ teaspoon red pepper flakes
- 1-2 tablespoon cornstarch
- sesame seeds (optional)
- ¼ cup Bourbon

DIRECTIONS

1. Salt & pepper chicken and place in freezer bag.
2. In a medium bowl, mix together honey, soy sauce, ketchup, oil, garlic, red pepper flakes, onion, bourbon and add to bag. Toss well to coat and freeze.
3. When ready place ingredients in crockpot and cook on low for 3-4 hours.
4. Combine 1 tablespoon cornstarch with 1 tablespoon water. Pour into crock pot & mix, If sauce doesn't thicken, add one more tablespoon of cornstarch and water. Stir around to coat.
5. Serve over rice, sprinkle with sesame seeds.

Southwestern Chicken Chili

6 servings

4-5 hours cooking time

INGREDIENTS

- 1½ pounds boneless chicken breast
- 3 cans petite diced tomatoes (14.5 ounces each)
- 2 cups medium salsa
- 1 (14.5 ounces) can corn, undrained
- 2 (14.5 ounces) cans black beans, drained and rinsed
- 1 package ranch seasoning
- 1 package taco seasoning
- Toppings - cheese, sour cream, tortilla strips, etc.

DIRECTIONS

1. Add all ingredients to a large freezer bag, toss well to coat and freeze.
2. When ready place ingredients in crockpot and cook on low for 4-5 hours.
3. Remove chicken from crock pot and shred. Place chicken back in crock pot and stir.
4. Serve with desired toppings.

Sausage & Peppers

6 servings

6-8 hours cooking time

INGREDIENTS

- 12-ounce package sausage, cut into ¼ in piece
- 1 green pepper, diced
- 1 red pepper, diced
- 1 small onion, diced
- 2 garlic cloves, minced
- 1 can Italian diced tomatoes
- 1 Tablespoon Italian seasoning

DIRECTIONS

1. Add all ingredients to a large freezer bag, toss well to coat and freeze.
2. When ready place ingredients in crockpot and cook on low for 6-8 hours.
3. Serve over rice.

Apple BBQ Pork Tenderloin

6 servings

6-8 hours cooking time

INGREDIENTS

- 1-2 pound pork tenderloin
- 1 cup chunky applesauce
- 1 cup BBQ sauce
- 2 tablespoon minced dried onion

DIRECTIONS

1. Add all ingredients to a large freezer bag, toss well to coat and freeze.
2. When ready place ingredients in crockpot and cook on low for 6-8 hours.
3. Serve over rice or pasta.

Pineapple Chicken Burritos

6 servings

6-8 hours cooking time

INGREDIENTS

- 1½ pounds boneless chicken breast
- ½ (20 ounces) can crushed pineapple, drained
- 1 (15 ounces) cans black beans, rinsed and drained
- 1 cups medium salsa
- 5-6 burrito sized flour tortillas
- 1 (10 ounce) cans green enchilada sauce
- 1 cups shredded cheddar
- 1 cup cooked rice

DIRECTIONS

1. Add all ingredients (except rice) to a large freezer bag, toss well to coat and freeze.
2. When ready place ingredients in crockpot and cook on low for 6-8 hours.
3. Remove the chicken and shred. Mix the chicken back into the crockpot with the rest of the ingredients.
4. Mix in the cooked rice.
5. Fill 5-6 of the burrito tortillas. Place in a 9×13 pan. Pour 1 can of the green enchilada sauce over the burritos.
6. Top with 1 cup of the shredded cheese and place under the broiler on the middle rack until the cheese is nice and melted. About 5 minutes.

Mongolian Beef

6 servings

4-5 hours cooking time

INGREDIENTS

- 1½ pounds beef flank steak, cut into strips
- 2 Tablespoon olive oil
- ½ Teaspoon minced ginger
- 2 Cloves garlic, minced
- ¾ cup soy sauce
- ¾ cup water
- ¾ cup brown sugar
- ¼ cup cornstarch
- ½ cup shredded carrots
- 3 med green onions, chopped

DIRECTIONS

1. Coat the beef flank steak in starch. Add all ingredients to a large freezer bag, toss well to coat and freeze.
2. When ready place ingredients in crockpot and cook on low for 4-5 hours.
3. Serve over rice or noodles.

Thai Peanut Chicken

6 servings

7-8 hours cooking time

INGREDIENTS

- 4 boneless, skinless chicken breasts
- 1 red pepper, diced
- 1 white onion, chopped
- ½ cup creamy peanut butter
- 1 lime, juiced
- ½ cup vegetable broth
- ¼ cup soy sauce
- ½ tablespoon cumin
- crushed peanuts for topping
- chopped scallions for topping
- cilantro for topping

DIRECTIONS

1. Add all ingredients (except toppings) to a large freezer bag, toss well to coat and freeze.
2. When ready place ingredients in crockpot and cook on low for 7-8 hours.
3. Serve over rice.
4. Top with peanuts, scallions, and cilantro.

Cheesy Chicken Spaghetti

6 servings

2-3 hours cooking time

INGREDIENTS

- 16-ounce spaghetti, cooked
- 1 pound Velveeta Light cheese
- 2 cups cooked, chopped chicken
- 1 can cream of mushroom soup
- 1 can cream of chicken soup
- 1 can petite diced tomatoes
- 1 4ounce can mild green chilies
- 1 cup mushrooms chopped
- ½ cup water
- 1 small onion, diced

DIRECTIONS

1. Add all ingredients to a large freezer bag, toss well to coat and freeze.
2. When ready place ingredients in crockpot and cook on low for 2-3 hours.
3. Enjoy!

Sweet Potato Basil Soup

6 servings

6-8 hours cooking time

INGREDIENTS

- 2 sweet potatoes or yams peeled and diced
- ½ yellow onion, sliced
- 1 14ounce coconut milk
- 1 cup vegetable broth
- 2 garlic cloves, minced
- 1 tablespoon dried basil
- salt & pepper, to taste

DIRECTIONS

1. Add all ingredients to a large freezer bag, toss well to coat and freeze.
2. When ready place ingredients in crockpot and cook on low for 6-8 hours.
3. Pour contents into blender or food processor and puree mixture until smooth.
4. Enjoy!

Mexican Pork and Sweet Potato Stew

5 servings

6-7 hours cooking time

INGREDIENTS

- 1 pound lean pork loin, cut into chunks
- 1 cup green chilies, diced
- ½ cups chicken broth
- 2 med sweet potatoes, peeled and cubed
- 1 med red onion, chopped
- 1 14.5 ounces can diced tomatoes, fire roasted
- ½ teaspoon cumin
- ½ teaspoon salt
- ¼ teaspoon pepper
- 1 tablespoon lime juice

DIRECTIONS

1. Add all ingredients (except lime) to a large freezer bag, toss well to coat and freeze.
2. When ready place ingredients in crockpot and cook on low for 6-7 hours.
3. Add lime juice and stir well.
4. Enjoy!

Cashew Chicken

6 servings

3-4 hours cooking time

INGREDIENTS

- 4 boneless, skinless chicken breasts
- ½ cup flour
- ½ teaspoon black pepper
- 1 tablespoon canola oil
- 3 tablespoon honey
- ¼ cup soy sauce
- 2 tablespoon rice wine vinegar
- 1 tablespoon brown sugar
- 1 garlic clove, minced
- ½ teaspoon grated ginger
- ¼ teaspoon red pepper flakes
- ½ cup cashews

DIRECTIONS

1. Combine flour and pepper in a large plastic bag, add chicken and toss to coat.
2. Heat oil in a skillet over medium heat and brown chicken for 2 minutes on each side, set aside to cool.
3. Whisk together honey, soy sauce, rice wine vinegar, brown sugar, garlic, ginger, and red pepper flakes and place in large freezer bag, add in chicken and seal closed. Place in the freezer.
4. When ready place ingredients in crockpot and cook on low for 3-4 hours.
5. Slice chicken and stir in cashews.
6. Serve over rice.

Cheesy Chicken Potato & Broccoli

6 servings

6 hours cooking time

INGREDIENTS

- 2-4 chicken breasts
- 1 large green pepper, chopped
- 2 cups broccoli, chopped
- 1 pound red potatoes, sliced thin
- 1 teaspoon paprika
- 1 can condensed cream of chicken soup
- ¼ pound VELVEETA cheese, cut into ½-inch cubes
- 1 tablespoon Worcestershire sauce
- ¼ cup chopped fresh parsley

DIRECTIONS

1. Add all ingredients (except cheese) to a large freezer bag, toss well to coat and freeze.
2. When ready place ingredients in crockpot and cook on low for 6 hours.
3. Add cheese and cook on high for additional 5 minutes. Stir.
4. Enjoy!

cho Chicken

servings

us cooking time

INGREDIENTS

- 2-4 chicken breast
- 1 can Rotel
- 1 package taco seasoning

DIRECTIONS

1. Add all ingredients to a large freezer bag, toss well to coat and freeze.
2. When ready place ingredients in crockpot and cook on low for 8-10 hours.
3. Spread Nacho Chicken over tortilla chips, and top with your choice of toppings including shredded cheese, green onions, black olives, lettuce, tomatoes, sour cream and salsa.

Black Bean and Corn Salsa Chicken

6 servings

7-8 hours cooking time

INGREDIENTS

- 2 (14 ounces) cans black beans, drained and rinsed
- 2 (14 ounces) cans corn, drained
- 1 (1 ounce) package taco seasoning
- 4-6 boneless chicken breasts
- 1 cup salsa
- ¾ cup water

DIRECTIONS

1. Add all ingredients to a large freezer bag, toss well to coat and freeze.
2. When ready place ingredients in crockpot and cook on low for 7-8 hours.
3. When finished cooking, shred chicken and serve over rice, with a salad, or in a wrap. Top with cheese, sour cream, avocado, lettuce, tomato.

Chicken Broccoli Alfredo

6 servings

4-6 hours cooking time

INGREDIENTS

- 4-6 boneless chicken breasts
- 1 (16 ounces) bag frozen broccoli florets
- 2 (16 ounces) jars Alfredo sauce (I use light)
- 1 large green pepper, chopped
- 1 (4 ounces) can sliced mushrooms, drained

DIRECTIONS

1. Add all ingredients to a large freezer bag, toss well to coat and freeze.
2. When ready place ingredients in crockpot and cook on low for 4-6 hours.
3. Enjoy!

Bacon-Feta Stuffed Chicken Breasts

6 servings

6-8 hours cooking time

INGREDIENTS

- 2 pounds chicken breasts, boneless/skinless
- 1/4 cup Feta cheese, crumbled
- 1/4 cup bacon, cooked and crumbled
- 2 (14.5 ounces) cans diced tomatoes, undrained
- 1 tablespoon basil

DIRECTIONS

1. In a small mixing bowl, combine the bacon pieces and the Feta cheese, mix well together.
2. Take each chicken breast and cut a slit (to form a pocket) on the thick side of the chicken breast. Don't cut all the way through.
3. Fill each pocket with a bit of the bacon/Feta mixture. Pinch shut the slit and secure with toothpicks or string. Place in a large freezer bag and freeze.
4. When ready, place the unthawed chicken breasts in the bottom of the crock pot. Pour in 2 cans of diced tomatoes, undrained and sprinkle the 1 tablespoon basil on top.
5. Cook on low 6-8 hours.
6. Serve and enjoy!

Beef Barley Stew

6 servings

8-10 hours cooking time

INGREDIENTS

- 2 pounds cubed beef
- 2 overflowing cups of baby carrots
- 1 envelope of Lipton onion soup mix
- 1 (29 ounces) can of beef broth
- 1 (14.5 ounces) diced tomatoes, with liquid
- 2 cups water
- 1 cup uncooked barley

DIRECTIONS

1. Add all ingredients (except barley) to a large freezer bag, toss well to coat and freeze.
2. When ready place ingredients in crockpot, add barley and cook on low for 8-10 hours.
3. Serve with a nice crusty bread and a side salad and enjoy!

Sweet & Sour Beef

6 servings

6-8 hours cooking time

INGREDIENTS

- 2 pounds of stir fry meat, cubed
- 1 bottle (10-12 ounce) sweet & sour sauce
- 1 cup of shredded carrots
- 2 tablespoons of shredded yellow onion, drained
- 4-6 cups of cooked rice
- one bag of stir fry veggies to cook in microwave or stove top.

DIRECTIONS

1. Cube meat beforehand and shred carrots beforehand as needed. Place all ingredients in the large freezer bag, except for rice & the bag of stir fry veggies. Freeze.
2. When ready place ingredients in crockpot and cook on low for 6-8 hours.
3. Right before the crockpot is done, cook rice on the stove top or rice cooker.
4. Cook stir-fry veggies in either the microwave or stove top.
5. Serve the sweet and sour beef over the stir fry veggies and rice.

Cheesy Potatoes and Ham

6 servings

6 hours cooking time

INGREDIENTS

- 28 ounces diced hash brown potatoes
- 2 cans of low sodium cream of mushroom
- 1 large yellow onion chopped
- 2 cans of water
- 2 ham steaks chopped
- 8 ounces of mild shredded cheddar cheese
- 4 cups of chopped broccoli
- 2 teaspoons of pepper
- order ingredients powered by chicory

DIRECTIONS

1. Add all ingredients to a large freezer bag, toss well to coat and freeze.
2. When ready place ingredients in crockpot and cook on low for 6 hours.
3. Enjoy!

Ham with Pineapple

6 servings

6-8 hours cooking time

INGREDIENTS

- 2 1/2 pounds ham
- 2 cans pineapple chunks, undrained
- Brown rice

DIRECTIONS

1. Add all ingredients to a large freezer bag, toss well to coat and freeze.
2. When ready place ingredients in crockpot and cook on low for 6-8 hours.
3. Serve over rice.

Carolina Style Pulled Pork Sandwiches

6 servings

8-9 hours cooking time

INGREDIENTS

- 3-pound Pork roast, boneless
- 1 tablespoon black pepper
- 1 tablespoon paprika
- 1 tablespoon salt
- 1 tablespoon brown sugar
- 1 cup cider vinegar
- 3/4 cup ketchup
- 2 tablespoon Worcestershire sauce
- buns

DIRECTIONS

1. Add all ingredients to a large freezer bag, toss well to coat and freeze.
2. When ready place ingredients in crockpot and cook on low for 8-9 hours.
3. Enjoy!

Barbecued Hamburgers

6 servings

5-6 hours cooking time

INGREDIENTS

- 3-4 pounds ground beef
- 2 (12 ounces) jars of beef gravy
- 1 cup chili sauce
- 1 cup ketchup
- 2 tablespoon Worcestershire sauce
- 2 tablespoon mustard
- buns

DIRECTIONS

1. Grill hamburger patties on grill or cook on your stovetop while getting the freezer bags ready. Divide all ingredients between 2 freezer bags, when hamburger patties are done, let cool a bit and then add to ingredients already in the bags. Do not add the buns or fries. Freeze
2. When ready place ingredients in crockpot and cook on low for 5-6 hours.
3. Enjoy!

Mediterranean Pork Chops

6 servings

7-8 hours cooking time

INGREDIENTS

- 6-8 pork chops, semi-thick cut
- 1/4 cup olive oil
- 2 cup chicken broth
- 4 cloves of garlic, chopped
- 2 tablespoon paprika
- 1 1/2 teaspoon poultry seasoning
- 2 teaspoon dried oregano
- 1 1/2 teaspoon dried basil

DIRECTIONS

1. Add all ingredients to a large freezer bag, toss well to coat and freeze.
2. When ready place ingredients in crockpot and cook on low for 7-8 hours.
3. Serve with rice or noodles.

Beefy Ravioli

6 servings

6-8 hours cooking time

INGREDIENTS

- 1 pound ground beef, cooked and drained
- 1 (24 ounces) jar spaghetti sauce
- 1 (25 ounces) bag frozen beef ravioli
- 1 cup mozzarella cheese, shredded

DIRECTIONS

1. Cook the ground beef until no longer pink, drain off grease if needed.
2. In a large bowl, open and dump the whole bag of frozen ravioli in it, next add the browned ground beef and the whole jar of spaghetti sauce. Mix well.
3. Put the mixed beefy ravioli mixture into a large freezer bag, zip shut and freeze.
4. When ready place ingredients in crockpot and cook on low for 6-8 hours.
5. Enjoy!

Hopin' John

6 servings

7-8 hours cooking time

INGREDIENTS

- 8 ounces slice smoked sausage
- 1 ¼ cups dice onion
- 1 cup diced carrot
- 1 ⅓ cups dice celery
- 30 ounces drain and rinse black-eyed peas, canned
- 10 ½ ounces diced tomatoes with green chilies
- 2 cups chicken broth, fat-free
- ¼ teaspoons Cajun seasoning

DIRECTIONS

1. Add all ingredients to a large freezer bag, toss well to coat and freeze.
2. When ready place ingredients in crockpot and cook on low for 7-8 hours.
3. Enjoy!

Coconut Tofu Curry

6 servings

4-5 hours cooking time

INGREDIENTS

- 10 fluid ounces light coconut milk, canned
- 1 tablespoon curry powder
- 2 tablespoons peanut butter, creamy
- 1 tablespoon Garam masala
- 2 cups chunk bell pepper, green
- 1 ½ teaspoons sea salt
- 8 ounces tomato paste
- 1 cup chunk onion
- 2 teaspoons minced garlic, cloves
- 1 cup diced tofu, firm

DIRECTIONS

1. Blend all ingredients except tofu in a food processor. Add all ingredients to a large freezer bag, toss well to coat and freeze.
2. When ready place ingredients in crockpot, add ½ cup water and cook on low for 4-5 hours.
3. Enjoy!

Stuffed Acorn Squash

6 servings

8 hours cooking time

INGREDIENTS

- 1 cup cook white rice, long-grain
- 2 cups drain and rinse lentils, brown, canned
- 1 tablespoon chop cranberries, dried
- 1 tablespoon chop pecans
- 1 teaspoon minced garlic, cloves
- 2 teaspoons chop thyme, fresh
- 1 teaspoon chop rosemary, fresh
- 1 tablespoon olive oil
- 1 individual squash, acorn
- ½ teaspoons salt
- ½ teaspoons black pepper

DIRECTIONS

1. In a mixing bowl, mix rice, lentils, chopped cranberries and pecans. Add garlic, thyme, rosemary and mix. Evenly brush olive oil over exposed flesh of acorn squash. Sprinkle with salt and pepper.
2. It may be necessary to cut a small slice off the bottom of the squash so it will lay flat. This will make it easier to fill, freeze and cook in the crockpot.
3. Stuff each squash half with rice mixture. Place each squash half in a baking dish and flash freeze. After frozen, place in freezer bag and freeze.
4. When ready place ingredients in crockpot, add ½ cup water and cook on low for 8 hours.
5. Enjoy!

Ginger Cranberry Pork Roast

6 servings

4-6 hours cooking time

INGREDIENTS

- 2 pork roasts, left whole
- 12-ounce package fresh cranberries
- 1 cup peeled and sliced fresh ginger
- 2 tablespoons honey
- 2 tablespoons of quick cooking tapioca

DIRECTIONS

1. Add all ingredients to a large freezer bag, toss well to coat and freeze.
2. When ready place ingredients in crockpot and cook on low for 4-6 hours.
3. Enjoy!

Healthy Mama BBQ Chicken

6 servings

4-6 hours cooking time

INGREDIENTS

- 3 medium unpeeled sweet potatoes cut into ½ inch pieces
- 2 large green peppers cut into strips or cubes
- 1 large red pepper cut into strips
- 2 zucchini chopped into circles 1 inch thick
- 2 cups chopped onion
- 2 tablespoon quick cooking tapioca
- 2 pounds chicken thighs or drumsticks
- 2 (15 ounces) jars of plain tomato sauce
- 4 tablespoons honey
- 2 tablespoons Worcestershire sauce
- 2 tablespoon ground yellow mustard
- 2 cloves garlic, finely minced
- 1 teaspoon salt

DIRECTIONS

1. Add all ingredients to a large freezer bag, toss well to coat and freeze.
2. When ready place ingredients in Crockpot and cook on low for 4-6 hours.
3. Serve with a salad and brown rice.

Three Packet Roast

6 servings

6-8 hours cooking time

INGREDIENTS

- 1 cup water
- 1 packet Italian-style salad dressing mix
- 1 packet ranch dressing mix (regular or buttermilk)
- 1 packet brown gravy mix
- 1 (3 pounds) boneless beef chuck roast

DIRECTIONS

1. Add all ingredients to a large freezer bag, toss well to coat and freeze.
2. When ready place ingredients in Crockpot and cook on low for 6-8 hours.
3. Enjoy!

Chicken Spaghetti

6 servings

6-8 hours cooking time

INGREDIENTS

- 4 boneless, skinless chicken breasts
- 14 ounce can crushed tomatoes
- 14 ounce can Italian seasoned diced tomatoes, undrained
- 1 green pepper, seeded & sliced thin
- 1 teaspoon oregano
- 1 teaspoon Italian seasoning
- kosher salt to taste
- 8 ounce cooked spaghetti (or any other pasta you have on hand)

DIRECTIONS

1. Add all ingredients to a large freezer bag, toss well to coat and freeze.
2. When ready spray the inside of your crock pot with non-stick spray and lay chicken breasts in the bottom.
3. Place ingredients in Crockpot and cook on low for 6-8 hours.
4. Enjoy!
5. Serve over hot cooked pasta.

Cowboy Casserole

4 servings

6-7 hours cooking time

INGREDIENTS

- ¼ cup diced onion
- ½ teaspoon pepper
- 1 teaspoon salt
- ½ teaspoon Mrs. Dash
- 1 pounds small red potatoes, sliced thin (about 4-5 small red potatoes),
- 1 can of cream of mushroom soup
- 1 pound ground beef browned and drained
- 1 can of diced tomatoes with liquid
- 1 cup canned corn, drained
- 1 can dark red kidney beans, drained
- 1 cup of shredded cheddar cheese (optional)

DIRECTIONS

1. Add all ingredients to a large freezer bag, toss well to coat and freeze.
2. When ready place ingredients in Crockpot and cook on low for 6-7 hours.
3. (Optional) Uncover crock-pot and sprinkle shredded cheese over top. Re-cover and let cook an additional 30 minutes.
4. Serve and enjoy!

Mexican Pulled Pork Tacos

6 servings

6-8 hours cooking time

INGREDIENTS

- 1 pound pork tenderloin
- 1 (15 ounces) can tomato sauce
- 1 tablespoon chili powder
- 1 teaspoon ground cumin
- 1 tablespoon brown sugar
- ½ teaspoon salt
- 3 cloves garlic, minced
- ½ teaspoon cayenne pepper (optional)
- 4 flour tortillas

DIRECTIONS

1. Add all ingredients to a large freezer bag, toss well to coat and freeze.
2. When ready place ingredients in Crockpot and cook on low for 6-8 hours.
3. When done, shred the pork using two forks, pulling against the grain of the meat.
4. Serve in warmed tortillas with optional toppings: shredded lettuce, sliced bell peppers, chopped tomatoes, black olives, grated cheddar cheese, and sour cream.

Ranch Pork Chops

6 servings

6-7 hours cooking time

INGREDIENTS

- 2 Cans Cream of Chicken soup
- 4-6 Pork Chops
- 1 packet Ranch

DIRECTIONS

4. Add all ingredients to a large freezer bag, toss well to coat and freeze.
5. When ready place ingredients in Crockpot and cook on low for 6-7 hours.
6. Enjoy!

Shredded Beef Tostada

6 servings

8-12 hours cooking time

INGREDIENTS

- 3 pounds beef roast
- 1 package Campbell's® Crockpot Sauces
- Shredded Beef Taco tostada shells
- shredded lettuce
- fresh salsa
- avocado
- sour cream
- cheese for toppings

DIRECTIONS

1. Add all ingredients to a large freezer bag, toss well to coat and freeze.
2. When ready place ingredients in Crockpot and cook on low for 8-12 hours.
3. Shred with two forks and serve over tostada shells and top with desired toppings.
4. Serve and enjoy!

Chicken Santa Fe

5 servings

5-6 hours cooking time

INGREDIENTS

- 1 (15 ounces) can black beans, rinsed and drained
- 2 (15 ounces) cans whole kernel corn, drained
- 1 cup bottled thick and chunky salsa, divided
- 5 or 6 skinless, boneless chicken breast halves
- 1 cup shredded Cheddar cheese

DIRECTIONS

1. Add all ingredients except cheese to a large freezer bag, toss well to coat and freeze.
2. When ready place ingredients in Crockpot and cook on low for 5-6 hours.
3. Sprinkle cheese on top, cover, and cook until the cheese melts, about 5 minutes.
4. Serve and enjoy!

Gone All Day Casserole

12 servings

6-8 hours cooking time

INGREDIENTS

- 1 cup uncooked wild rice, rinsed and drained
- 1 cup chopped celery
- 1 cup chopped carrots
- 2 (4 ounces) cans mushroom stems and pieces, drained
- 1 large onion, chopped
- 1 garlic clove, minced
- 1/2 cup slivered almonds
- 3 beef bouillon cubes
- 2 1/2 teaspoons seasoned salt
- 2 pounds boneless round steak, cut into 1-inch cubes
- 3 cups water

DIRECTIONS

1. Add all ingredients to a large freezer bag, toss well to coat and freeze.
2. When ready place ingredients in Crockpot and cook on low for 6-8 hours.
3. Enjoy!

Russian Apricot Chicken

6 servings

8 hours cooking time

INGREDIENTS

- 1 (12 ounces) jar of apricot preserves
- 1 bottle of Russian salad dressing
- 1 to 2 pounds boneless, skinless chicken breasts
- 1/2 onion, chopped

DIRECTIONS

1. Add all ingredients to a large freezer bag, toss well to coat and freeze.
2. When ready place ingredients in Crockpot and cook on low for 8 hours.
3. Serve with rice or mashed potatoes and enjoy!

Caribbean Chicken

6 servings

4-6 hours cooking time

INGREDIENTS

- 2 pounds chicken breasts
- 8 ounce can pineapple chunks with juice
- 1/4 cup packed brown sugar
- 1/2 teaspoon nutmeg
- 1/3 cup orange juice
- 1/2 cup raisins

DIRECTIONS

1. Add all ingredients to a large freezer bag, toss well to coat and freeze.
2. When ready place ingredients in Crockpot and cook on low for 4-6 hours.
3. Enjoy!

Conclusion

Thank you for reading. If you want to read my other books you can go to Amazon and check out my author page.

If you've enjoyed this book, I would like you to leave a positive review on Amazon because it would be very helpful. If you want to add something or have some suggestions write them down.

FREE eBook: 7 Steps to Health and the Big Diabetes Lie

Learn about the shocking drug-free disease destroying methods that have been hidden and suppressed by big pharma for decades.

FOR A FREE DOWNLOAD

GO TO http://bit.ly/1PmCo5m

Thank you and enjoy!

81290762R00130

Made in the USA
Columbia, SC
19 November 2017